MAUI CHILD

MAUI CHILD

Barbara Bown Robinson

drawings
Peg M. Frazer

Press Pacifica

Library of Congress Cataloging-in-Publication Data

Robinson, Barbara Bown.
Maui Child.

1. (Hawaii)—Poetry. 2. Robinson, Barbara—Bown—Biography—Youth. 3. Poets, American—20th century—Biography. 4. Maui (Hawaii)—Social life and customs. 1. title. PS3568.028M3 1987 811'.54
86–30300

ISBN 0–916630–51–X (pbk.)

Illustrated by Peg M. Frazer

Grateful acknowledgment is made to the following publications in which some of the articles and poems in this book appeared earlier.

"ALOHA, THE MAGAZINE OF HAWAII AND THE PACIFIC: "Kimono Day";
AMERICAN POETRY ANTHOLOGY: "Inheritance Taxes";
HONOLULU: "Plantation Theater Arts";
LATITUDE 20: "Quilting Lesson," and "Sikorsky".

Typeset by The Last Word, Kailua, Hawaii.

Printed in the United States of America.

Available from:
Press Pacifica, P.O. Box 47, Kailua,
Oahu, Hawaii 96734.

FOREWORD

Edith Hamilton once said, "We live in the ever present past." On Maui, this new-old island of myth and high rises, we see this clearly all around us.

Each evening with the sunset the purple shadow of the ancient West Maui Mountains rises against the younger slopes of Haleakala.

Geometric angles of new many-storied hotels and condominiums spring up along the long shores of Kihei and Makena where, I remember, there were only twelve homes, and where the beach was sprinkled with cowrie shells along the high-tide line. And the Puunene winds, and the reefs and tides, and phosphorescence on the star-lit sands, and seasons of shark and whale and bird, were things to be reckoned with. And a trip between the islands began on one day and ended on the next.

Today, we fly from one island to another in forty minutes, and with an automobile on the Haleakala road, we can pass through several climates and geographical stages in less than two hours. Starting at the sea-level marshes near Kahului, we drive on through the cane lands of Puunene, up through pineapple country into the upland ranch lands of Makawao and Kula. On up through the elevations of fog and cloud the forest is tall and fragrant, but at still higher altitudes, the trees dwindle to *ohelo* and fern, until vegetation disappears almost entirely at the cindery summit where solar observatories track our planetary route around the sun.

Easy highways override the dust and jolts of the old roads. Even so, the old ways of this island are everpresent.

And so in these pages, though time, courtesy, and capricious memory have obscured names and sequence, bright images of these very real Maui people and echoes of these happenings of my child time, are with me still.

TABLE OF CONTENTS

PEG FRAZER

RELATIVITY

One day when I was a little kid
my mom played baseball with us.
Crack!
She smacked a homer
off my best pitch
right over the *naupaka* bush
and past the birdbath
in Aunt Winnie's yard.

Even so
I thought she was too old
to be running around the bases
like that, her skirts
flipping up over her knees

while my grandmother
made tatting lace
in the shade of the *milo* tree,
and cheered my mom
as she raced toward home plate
instead of telling her
to act her age.

And yet, today–
I'm older than my grandmother was then,
and my mother was younger then
than my daughter is
now.

Strange how
I don't feel as old now,
as I thought my mother was
then.

LAHAINA LANDING

One moon-bright midnight, long before airplanes began carrying us in comfort from one island to another, I struggled from our stateroom onto the heaving deck of the Inter-Island Steamship *Hualalai*. Gripping the salt-sticky railing, I peered out at the huge waves sweeping shoreward and could feel the change in the rhythm of the ship's engine. It was running now at dead slow ahead, just enough, I was told, to keep headway against the *Alanuihaha* current.

Our ship, enroute from Honolulu to Hilo, was pausing outside Maui's reefs to let five passengers disembark at Lahaina Roads. Three of these were my mother, myself, and my tenth birthday–gift kitten.

Two men lurched past me. I listened to them clomping down the deck and squinted through the dark toward the distant wharf. Dad would be there. He'd be waiting on the lantern-lit planks standing amidst the stacks of molasses-smelling sugar bags, rows of mysterious crates, and curvy heaps of fishing nets.

To reach that dock, we were preparing to cross a mile of rough sea in an open boat.

From where I watched, I saw it coming to meet us. The open whaler with its four oarsmen seemed fragile as a paper cup as it spidered over the whitecapped rollers, disappearing in the trough before each wave sweeping toward it, reappearing each time in a burst of spray.

Near me at the railing, the sailors were already helping the clumpy-shoed men through the gangplank gate. And now, here along the windy deck came my Mother, clutching my Persian kitten, an impulse gift from a Honolulu aunty. Of course we wanted the kitten, but *auwe!* somehow his basket had vanished during the night. Handing me her purse, Mother tucked the angry kitten inside the front of her dress, and together we too lurched to the gang-plank gate where the sailors were waiting for us.

One at a time, we backed through the rail-gate to the narrow top step of an iron ladder that had been let down against the side of the ship's hull.

Strong brown men, clinging to the ladder's chains, passed us from hand to hand, down the ladder to a yard-wide gridiron platform that hung, grinding and shuddering against the hull.

There we waited, my kitten yowling his fury at inter-island travel from inside Mother's blouse.

With each ponderous roll to port, the ladder shrieked in its shackles, its platform swaying out over the swash and slap of the waves. As the ship groaned back, then heeled to starboard, the ladder clanged in a long rippling crash against the iron plates of the hull. Adding to this clamor were the separate sounds of wind shrieking in the rigging, tarpaulins clapping over crates and bales, passengers retching over the stern rail, mules hee-hawing in the hold, and the yells and whistles of greeting between the oarsmen and the ship's crew.

An enormous swell lifted the whaleboat smoothly to Mother's feet, and with her usual dignity, she stepped in, and was seated behind two oarsmen.

My turn. Flappy pleated dress, bumpy purses, whippy hair, all slapping me in the gale; tight as a squid, I cowered against the rust-smelling ladder, one hand clenched on a slippery chain, the other gripping the rope belt of the crewman who stood loose as a trapeze artist beside me.

Up swept the boat again, and the cliff-like iron-riveted hull dipped down to meet it.

"Eeeeeeeeyoh-Sho!" sang out the acrobat beside me, and I was plucked from the ladder and flung across the foaming thrash. Smack! and I was safely clamped against the hard, smooth, wet, friendly chest of a laughing Hawaiian giant. My first real hero.

My hero plopped me down onto the plank seat in front of him, and swung out a long oar. I heard the kitten's growls and knew Mother was on a seat behind us. Two wet bundles in the prow turned out to be the two clumpy-shoed men.

The oarsmen thunked their oars in the locks, and casually swirled the boat away.

As we left the shelter of the *Hualalai,* the waves swooped

upon us, higher than the standing steersman. All the men shouted at once. *"Hui! Hui! Hui! Hui!"* They bent to the oars with mighty sweeps. A mountain of hissing comber lifted our boat and flung us forward, the men shouting and laughing, and in long lunges and slides we swept toward the shore.

We crossed the roaring distance, foamed over the reef and sloshed onward toward the wharf, just barely afloat.

And there was Dad. From where I sat, soaked and shivering, his familiar starched-white-suited figure beckoned like a candle on the moonlit pier.

The oarsmen lashed ropes fore and aft, and boosted the two men over the gunwale to some steep dark steps.

Dad stepped down. He gave money to the boat men, his hand to Mother, a frosty glance to the kitten. He looked down at me, still gripping the gunwale, huddled against my hero, and laughed. Then I was swung up between them like a bag of poi.

Far out beyond the breakers, the *Hualalai,* looking like a diamond-belted caterpillar, dipped and bowed, and hooted goodbye.

Dad took off his crisp white coat. Bending, he wrapped it around me. I said goodbye to my regal mariner friend, and dripped off to our Essex touring car (no glassed windows) for the two-hour drive from Lahaina to Wailuku.

THE FLOWER LADIES

The flower lady used to stop at our house.
"Foorawah!" she'd shout.
And my mother would take her shabby purse
and go out to the bench under the mango tree.
There the bent old woman would squat under
her worn-smooth *huki*-pole, and lower two huge bamboo
baskets to the ground.

Every week the thin sweaty woman would arrive,
often as I, in sharply-ironed white shorts,
was leaving for a game of tennis.
A shallow ignoramus I was. Self-ordained martyr,
I resented my mother's wave
sending me back to the kitchen to fetch
two glasses and the pink teapot full of lemonade.

We were poor, I thought then,
too poor for two cars, and I,
sulking, had to walk to the playground.
And yet, every week it was like this–
my mother carrying her open purse
to the flower lady.

She'd always take ages, my mother would,
lifting out bundles of flowers,
lingering longest over the saffron-blue-brown
bouquets of smiling pansy faces;
each in its basket of freshly plaited
cool green *ti*-leaf.

They'd share the seeds Mrs. Lyman sent from Hilo.
And talk of aphids, and rain, and chicken *manua*.
And at last mother would select two large bunches,
long sprangly stalks of gladiolus,
or oozy bundles of raggedy iris,
string-wrapped in cornucopias of soggy newspaper.

One day I put her small blue
Wedgewood bowl on the sink,
thinking, if she had any sense,
she'd take the hint.
But no.
That week as usual,
there was the heap of awkward stalks
she always managed somehow to arrange.

"You know pansies are your favorite,"
I scolded one day.
"Why must you always choose
the gawkiest things in her basket?"

My mother stared at me, amazed.
"They're the heaviest," she explained,
gently, as though I hadn't a brain in my head.

Strange how blind I remained.
I never perceived their mutual courtesy
until the day I saw the Flower Lady stoop,
at my mother's funeral, and set on the ground
two tiny bouquets
of brown, gold and blue pansy faces
each in its basket of freshly plaited
cool green *ti*-leaf.

P.M.E.

THE MUD FENCE

"Homely as a mud fence," my mother once said of Great-aunt Winnie. I looked at her then in surprise. My mother said that? She who never said a mean thing about anyone in her life?

"Homely," she'd said again. "Not ugly. And there's nothing dull about mud fences. You think about it."

Well, I thought about mud fences and about Aunt Winnie. Knowing how precise my mother was about words, it was a puzzle.

"I thought homely meant ugly," I'd protested.

"Not ugly," she'd insisted.

Eventually, since the problem remained knotty I tried coming at it from another direction.

What might be the opposite of homely? Cute? Pretty? Suave, svelte, chic, slick, stylish? How about sophisticated? Supercilious?

I thought more about Aunt Winnie. Absolutely she was NOT any of these. Actually, come right down to it, she wasn't definitely anything in particular. She was kind of squarish; hair kind of brownish-grey, cut sort of middlish. Mouth, ears, and eyes big but not very; nose small but not cute. She didn't laugh a lot and tell jokes, or raise dogs or drive a big car. So what was there to think about?

Even her little house next door was ordinary. Just grassy paths between yellow, pink, and red hibiscus hedges and middle-sized avocado trees, and guava and mulberry bushes full of ordinary birds. And bird-feeders hanging just any old where.

But her front door was always open, and her fat yellow cat slept on her piano, and walked up and down the keys when Aunt Winnie played "The Happy Farmer" or "Humoresque." And sometimes Aunt Winnie and I played "Chopsticks" very fast, our four hands making big chords to fool him as he pounced about on the keys, chase-patting our fingers and purring and us both laughing.

And then we'd go into her kitchen where Emmeline the big brown spider (great, great, ever so great, granddaughter of Charlotte, who spun words like "humble" in her web) lived behind Aunt Winnie's clock. Just an ordinary spider though, who didn't spin any kind of web.

From the biggish square glass jar, Aunt Winnie would take out four lumpy mango-chutney cookies, and we'd put on our big clacky wooden *geta* and go out in the woodsy part of her garden where it was cool, and where all sorts of birds were feasting on the guavas and mulberrys. And we'd just sit, and watch, and nibble; not talking much, just quietly enjoying the afternoon together.

Between us and the pasture was a low humpy wall with a lot of tomato plants and a potato vine, and ferns and a jillion kinds of flowering weeds growing all over it. All sorts of everyday kinds of little creatures buzzed over, ran along, or dug into this wall, and I always pushed myself around so I could watch them too. I'd see red ants, and dragonflies, snails, Hilo spiders, crab spiders, beetles, gekkos, skinks, and sometimes a brown mouse. In a couple of bare spots, some sparrows scratched teacup-wide holes in the dirt, and took dust baths there, while the yellow cat gave them the big ignore through the dining room window.

There was something different happening there all the time, though never anything spectacular. But one day, watching Aunt Winnie poke seeds into a soft patch, I got curious about the wall itself.

"Aunty, is that an old Hawaiian wall?"

"Oh no. It's just a mud fence. Shoveled it up myself long ago during a rainy season. Keeps the cows out of my mulberry bushes."

Then came a day my daughter came to me. She was almost the age I was then, a gawky skinny child. She had made leis of hibiscus for herself and Hildegaard, her ugly black puppy, and paraded herself before me. "Amen't I pretty?"

I look at her carefully. Ears, eyes, feet, too big. Straggly brownish hair, lop-toothed grin.

Homely as a mud fence, I started to tell myself but

stopped, remembering the nasturtiums, the birds and orchids and parsley, the flowering weeds, and the brown mouse and the dragonflies, and the countless other marvels that I associate still with Aunt Winnie and her mud fence.

"You look just right," I said, noticing that her gaze shifted to my empty square glass cookie jar. "Not too fancy for a little messy work. Want to help me make some mango-chutney cookies?"

QUILTING LESSON

One day, long before airplanes came to Maui, my mother's new mail order quilt arrived by ship from California.

Great-aunt Winne came through the hedge to see. "You call that a real quilt?" There it lay brave and bright, still latticed with fold creases from its packing. She lifted a corner and let it drop. "Tuh!"

"Why do you say "Tuh!" I asked.

Some days later Aunt Winnie took me with her to explain. We started out in her courageous red Ford roadster, rumble-seat model, drove through Wailuku town, turned left toward Olowalu, then right up a steep valley until the road dwindled into a trail, left wheels on the main rut, right wheels tracking along as best they could through brush and *pili* grass. Eventually the trail split into faint diverging paths, one going on up the valley, the other downhill in the direction of Kihei Beach.

Aunt Winnie calmly stopped the car, stepped out and clambered up a stony bank. No simple climb for anyone, but Aunt Winnie, nearly seventy years old, had curiously bent feet, all cramped from arthritis.

Up I came. But there was no house in sight, just a series of taro ponds, the young taro plants at our feet shading schools of tiny fish. Narrow stone and sod walls made causeways, framing the taro patches, separating them into irregular shapes, like uneven steps going up along the bottom of the valley.

Aunt Winnie straightened her back, took a deep breath, and hobbled off in her lopsided gait. It hardly seemed those crippled feet could carry her safely along the narrow paths between the ponds. But after a bit I discovered I'd better watch my own feet.

At every intersection between patches we had to hurdle a wooden watergate. Up and up, deeper into the narrowing valley we went until it seemed the green cliffs leaned over us.

Then suddenly Aunt Winnie stopped. She tipped her head back. "Ey-oh, Looolee!" she called.

From somewhere farther up came an invisible reply. "Ey-oh!" a voice sang.

We climbed a last terrace, and found rocky steps going up to a house– a real house with red corrugated-iron roof, and a wide lanai, framed by towering mango trees.

A whiskey-brown dog ambled down to meet us. Ducks woke up and squawked off to the nearest taro pond, and we climbed to a stone-paved landing. Aunt Winnie pointed to a mossy bamboo flume pouring its small stream into a giant white clamshell. There I washed my feet. Aunt Winnie removed her shoes, and with clean bare feet we ascended three wide plank steps and stood together on a long *lauhala* mat, smooth and pale as ivory.

"Aloha, Wini!" the voice called. "My heart is happy you are here."

"Aluli, aloha!" replied my great-aunt.

"Ah, I see you bring one fine *keiki. Hele mai,* you two. Come in. Come in."

Close behind Aunt Winnie I walked across the lanai, my eyes still adjusting to the deep shade.

There she was, seated on a wicker settee, a round graceful woman with eyes and voice that mixed tears and smile together as she held Aunt Winnie's hand to her cheek. Then she held out her arms to me. Her hair smelled of fresh ginger blossoms and my hands felt comfortable in hers.

After a moment she looked up and beckoned. "Liliana," she called. *"Hele mai!"*

From somewhere in the house a young girl appeared and looked at us from a doorway.

"See, Lili, here is Wini, and a friend for you."

Then the girl nodded and laughed silently. Anyway it seemed she was laughing—both hands held before her face.

"Run, Liliana, and bring!" said the lady.

Liliana ran. She returned with a long bulky roll carried lightly in her arms. With a kind of careful, bird-like swoop, she laid it on the floor before the lady and stepped back.

We made a square there, the bundle on the floor, the four of us spaced around it.

Then the lady lifted both arms in a classic hula benediction. "And now," she said, "you will see."

Aunt Winnie seated herself quietly on the mat, tucking her feet under her wide pleated skirt. Her silver hair seemed luminescent in the shadowy room, but under her fierce dark eyebrows, I knew her eyes were blue as the ocean at noon. She darted a glance at me and I sat.

Liliana unrolled the long bundle, patting and smoothing it, until there it lay, a marvelous quilt, green and brown on white, a strong exciting design of breadfruit branches and leaves.

Wordlessly we admired it. Curving rows of tiny stitches echoed the design.

"What makes it so soft." I asked at last. "My mother has a new quilt. But it's heavy and hard." An angry quack sounded from below the stairs.

The lady laughed. *"Ae!* The ducks answer you. The ducks give the soft underneath feathers. Then they go away plenty *huhu,* angry, to grow some more."

"Must take a million feathers," I said.

"Ae. But such a quilt lies over you soft like the cloud. And here we have many ducks. Liliana, go show the ducks."

Liliana rose and moved toward the steps. I followed eagerly. The small brown dog joined us. Together we explored the caves behind curtains of *lilikoi* vines. We admired tiny fish in the stream, ate mountain apples from the steep shady forest, gathered many kinds of ferns and flowers and made a *haku* lei. And we laughed and laughed as we tried to count the ducks. All too soon we were called back to the lanai where our two aunties were talking of another new quilt.

Liliana took me to the far end of the lanai and we ran our hands over the straight smooth guava logs that made the quilt frame. Needles and thread and two logs on trestles. That was all the equipment there was.

Aunt Winnie shook out a white cloth sack. Big letters on it spelled out WAILUKU SUGAR CO. We folded the quilt into a big puffy square and tucked it into the sack.

"Hardly weighs a pound," Aunt Winnie said. "We'll take turns carrying it."

Once more I stood before the stately Hawaiian lady, my hands in hers. Then we went down the steps and along the narrow paths that rimmed the taro ponds, and down the steep bank to the little red car. Aunt Winnie backed the car a long way until there was a wide place to turn around.

"Is she a queen?" I asked.

"She's a princess, and an artist."

"I thought a princess was supposed to be rich."

"All she owns is this valley. She hasn't a dime to spend."

I glanced over to see Aunt Winnie's smile. But she wasn't joking. Her hands were clenched on the steering wheel and her face looked strangely sad.

As we arrived home, Haleakala was glowing pink in the sunset. Aunt Winnie choked off the engine and we sat silently gazing out across Kahului. The shadow of the West Maui Mountains flowed across the land. Like a slow purple wave it rose, steadily extinguishing the diamond-like flashes reflectting from the glass windows in the still sunlit homes on the Kula slopes of the great mountain.

At last I spoke again. "Is she truly an artist?"

"This quilt is a masterpiece."

We stepped carefully from the muddy car and Aunt Winnie let me carry the quilt into her living room and spread it out on her big *pune'e*.

One day soon after, a doctor-uncle arrived. "What!" he said. "Way up that muddy valley just for a quilt? And waiting for it a whole year?"

Aunt Winnie smiled serenely.

"But, Win!" He shook some white pills from an envelope and put them on her table. "You could order a dozen quilts from San Francisco. Quicker and cheaper. And you're certainly not helping your feet clambering up those donkey trails."

He went into her kitchen and returned with a glass of water. "Now I hear you're planning to hobble all the way back there again, lugging more materials, like a delivery boy?" He put the glass next to her pills. "Even though you and Luli, old school chums and all that . . . feet like yours . . . is it worth it?"

Aunt Winnie reached out to the *pune'e* beside her and lifted the quilt toward her. Light as a cloud it lay across her knees. Gently her gnarled finger traced the edge of a minutely stitched border. She didn't say a word, but when her glance met mine, I knew I'd be seeing my friend Liliana again.

SENSEI

When I was a small, ratty kid
Mieko-*san* lived with us.
She was only our maid, I'd say,
when I was small.
She washed the dishes,
and our dirty clothes
and washed out my mouth
with yellow Fels Naptha soap
when I said bad words.

Then, one day
I climbed on the kitchen table
and looked down at her and said,
"When I get big,
I'll be rich and wise.
And you'll look up at me
and not boss me any more,
cause then you'll know
I'm somebody important."

But Mieko-*san,* who spoke two languages,
though little in mine,
lifted me down
and said,

> "When high on tall tree
> red gold mango look most big,
> small people throw stone."

She didn't say it exactly that way.
She said it in her own sounds,
and I didn't understand why she said it,
but the music of those lines sang in my mind
and I asked her to write her words, her way.

She did.

Three vertical rows of *hirogana*
in black, black ink
on transluscent rice paper.

As I grew older
I struggled to learn the Japanese alphabet,
and I listened to what she'd say
as I helped her wash dishes,
and began to understand why bigger
is not the same as wiser.

And today?

Today
I call her
Sensei.

KIMONO DAY

For Mieko-*san*, and for all of us, it was kimono day once again and we watched the dawning skies anxiously even though Mieko confidently expected sunshine and quiet. She was right every year. And every year this increased my awe of her, and of her Buddha—so unfailingly gracious.

On this morning I watched my always-in-a-hurry father as he eased the old Essex sedan out of the garage and drove so slowly down the sandy driveway that no puff of dust was raised. My mother walked after the car, dragged the two screeching wings of the tall iron gate closed, clanged the long bar down, and locked it with a filigreed iron key. For this one day of the year, no cars would come farther up the road than to Aunt Winnie's house. Furthermore, all balls, tricycles, and scooters were locked up in the storeroom. Not a single speck of dust was to be stirred up today.

Mieko's husband Rokero-*san* had the day off even though the pineapple canning season was in full swing. The neighborhood children on this one day were kept away. But my sister and I had permission to watch from the kitchen sidewalk, knowing that if we put even one toe off that freshly washed walkway we'd be sent straight indoors.

We could watch from the upstairs windows to be sure, but there was more to this affair than just watching.

In the dim dawn two of Rokero's brothers and their wives arrived and parked their car outside the gate. Quietly the brothers stretched long ropes between our house-roof eaves and a tall *kiawe* tree across the lawn. Aunt Winnie, Mrs. Rowan, and my grandmother arrived through the hedge carrying rolls of *lauhala* and grass *tatami* mats from their bedrooms, and the two brothers laid them out under the lines and over the lawn, creating a patchwork-quilt effect of matting from all our houses. Not an inch of our sloping front lawn was left uncovered, and a long path of *lauhala* matting led to the door of Mieko's and Rokero's cottage.

Aunt Winnie and my mother turned on garden hoses and wet down the ground in Aunt Winnie's garden and in our papaya grove and chicken pen. Mr. Douglas next door turned on the sprinklers over his sandy back yard where no grass grew, and Rokero and his brothers went into the garage and brought up, one by one, three great pine chests with rope handles and brass fittings, and placed them in a long row on the mats. Then Rokero and his brothers went, stepping carefully along the *lauhala* path, into the cottage.

As the clouds were turning pink over Iao Valley they came out again, dressed now in trim dark kimono with tight black sashes.

Next Rokero's sisters-in-law emerged from the cottage. They were dressed in beautiful gray kimono with *obi* of orange, green and gold patterns on white satin. Silently they held the door open and quietly Mieko appeared.

Each year, at this moment, she became transformed once more into a distant mysterious other self; someone, we eventually learned, who appeared on this day once again the person she really was, the daughter of a noble family in Hiroshima. She had arrived in Hawaii with her husband, a political refugee, to become, at the age of forty, a servant in a foreign household.

Mieko never clashed with anyone. But no one ever argued with her either. Even with broom or vegetable peeler in hand, she was never ordinary, never without dignity. As my grandmother said, "A real lady never needs to say she's a lady."

Now Mieko paused in the early sunlight, regal in her stiff court robe of gold, red, silver, and black. There she stood, framed by pink oleander, the garage wall, hibiscus hedges, jacaranda and *kiawe* trees, green lawn and lavender sky.

Haleakala was on her left, the West Maui Mountains to her right. Aunt Winnie's best *lauhala* mat was under her feet. Before her ran the soft woven paths connecting her with these families of Hawaii and England and Japan and America who now waited before her.

Aunt Winnie stood near a hibiscus bush marking a dimly remembered boundary between her yard and ours. She held four quilted coat hangers. I knew she kept those special hangers for her San Francisco clothes, and that right now those coats and dresses were draped over a chair in her bedroom. My mother also waited, also holding her best hangers, wooden ones covered with grandmother's crocheted wool webbing. Mother's party dresses were tossed on her bed today, as were those belonging to Mrs. Rowan.

Mieko looked over her court, a far cry from the hundred servants and the gardens of her own family estate in Hiroshima. No one spoke. No one moved. It was a sad, grand moment for all of us.

At last Mieko moved up the gently rising slope to where the three men waited. She gave her husband a tiny nod. Then Rokero and his two brothers bowed in old-fashioned style to her, turned to the first big chest and lifted the heavy creaking lid.

Perfumes of spices and camphor rose and flowed around us, mingling with the ever-present scents of lantana and gardenia.

The two sisters stepped closer. Rokero stooped and lifted out a glimmering roll of red and silver brocade and laid it carefully across the outstretched arms of the two sisters. Slim tubes of soft packing were drawn from inside the roll which, unfolded, became a magnificent kimono. The kimono was set upright, so stiff with silver thread embroidery that it stood alone, unsupported, brave and unsagging before Mieko.

After a long pause, she walked slowly around it, inspecting without touching. Returning to her position facing the robe, she nodded again to Rokero.

Carefully, he slid his hand through a cuff, drawing the wing-like sleeve, collar and other sleeve up toward his shoulder until the kimono hung like a banner from his extended arm. He swayed left, swayed right, then with smooth powerful grace, turned himself in wide circles; and the robe, rising like a heavy, crimson kite, sailed rustling and sparkling in the slanting sun beams, filling the morning air with the scent of cedar.

It seemed alive—a great slow-flying moth.

With gentle precise movements Rokero brought it to rest, poised on his arm. He glanced toward Aunt Winnie, and she put a soft cushioned hanger in his hand.

Swiftly, lightly, Rokero floated the kimono onto the hanger and again lifted it high. The two sisters fixed big ivory fasteners to close the front, and the robe was hung up on the pole-braced line to sway in the breeze.

At a nod from Mieko, another kimono was lifted from the chest. This one was pink with silver embroidery, lined with darker pink. After a flight on Rokero's arm it was arranged on one of mother's hangers and hung up on the rope, two arm-span's distance from the first.

As each marvelous kimono was lifted from the chest, its rolls of inner padding were carefully arranged on the open lid. The silk box lining was lifted and draped over the edge, and the chest and its trays were left open to the sun.

One by one, each shimmering kimono was lifted out: patterns of butterflies, peacocks, bamboo, plum blossoms, leaves, buds and chrysanthemums in crimson, green, lavender, rose, ivory, and black, each kimono stiff with the weight of silk, gold, and silver thread. Twenty noble garments were taken from the chests, placed erect and separate on the mat, lifted, floated, and set to sway and swoop on the high pole-braced lines.

The sun rose higher and the breeze became a wind that swept up from the plains of Kahului. Mr. Douglas turned the sprinklers higher over his sandy yard.

Aunt Winnie and Rokero's brothers walked through the hibiscus hedge to her lanai and brought back her tall curvy peacock chair. The chair was placed in the shade of the *kiawe* tree. Mieko was seated and a yard-square flat cushion was placed under her feet. Her sisters brought her tea in tiny cups while the treasured garments from her child-home swayed like courtiers before her.

And all that day Mieko dreamed, until the evening shadows of the West Maui Mountains rose inexorably up the pink slopes of Haleakala. Then her families came again, wrapped each kimono in silk once more, and lowered them, one by one, into their chests.

Ropes and poles and mats were taken away.

As the sunset faded into grey, the chests were closed, and carried down the sloping lawn to be stacked once more, one on top of the other, against a wall in our dark, dusty garage.

SIKORSKY

As our Sikorsky amphibious aircraft slid down the sky, lower and nearer the water, my mother reached across the narrow aisle and patted my knee. "Don't be scared," she said.

Who could be scared I wondered. I was almost eleven years old and my first airplane trip was pure miracle. Of course, I knew about the magic turbanned Djinns of Arabia. So they could fly over deserts on their flying carpets? Hah! I was flying from Maui over blue ocean—Carter's ink blue. And close approaching was Oahu with its two ridgy mountains skirted by canefields and bordered by white surf.

Down we went, still closer to the water. A pink palace passed by almost beside us. Mother said it was the Royal Hawaiian Hotel. Lower we went. Lower and slower and louder. The wave tops seemed almost parallel with our windows.

Then suddenly we nosed up slightly, and with a mighty SAHWOOOOOSH . . . we were like a fat scimitar cleaving the ocean surface.

The sea folded up around us, displaying inside it a glimpse of coral and darting things and then flung us up to rock on its surface.

I remained glued to the splashy window scene, blinking at the alternating views of mountains and waves, then noticed, in between, that a couple of outrigger canoes were paddling toward us.

Three seats ahead of me the pilot was clicking switches and turning knobs. The propellers along the top wing stopped turning and I could hear the water slapping against the sides of our cigar-shaped hull. The pilot rose, squeezed down the aisle between the twelve passengers, climbed a steep ship's ladder, and disappeared through a hatch in our cabin ceiling.

One by one the other passengers wrestled themselves out of their seats and up the ladder and climbed through the hatch. Gentlemen first, for reasons of modesty, my mother explained; the ladies, clutching their skirts, last.

Then it was my turn to grip my way down the aisle toward the tail. Though I was used to the ponderous heave and roll of the inter-island steamships *Hualalai* and *Waialeale,* this twisty flouncing wind-wave motion made me think of Jonah inside the indignant whale.

I emerged from the hatch. The pilot guided my feet down a series of metal footrests until I stood balancing on the lower wing, clinging to a slanting wing-brace. The first canoe, with four passengers, was already bobbing off toward the dock while two paddlers were maneuvering the second canoe, like a sideways battering ram, close alongside. The pilot, using some of the interesting words I'd learned on troublesome cattle drives, was warding off the canoe with his foot.

Passengers leaped and flopped from airplane to canoe. Then I was slung over to the front paddler, and parked in the prow, wedged against a sack of sweet potatoes.

Off we went at a leisurely pace, to be met at a wooden dock by an uncle bearing leis.

After what seemed a long drive past rice fields, then through dusty Honolulu town, Uncle swung his Ford roadster wide to miss the open-sided trolley, and turned right from King street down Kalakaua Avenue toward Waikiki. More rice fields and taro ponds, smelling of ducks and mud, were punctuated with tall coconut palms and water buffalo. We bounced along Kalakaua close to narrow, gritty Waikiki beach, then turned *mauka* for half a block, and there was grandmother's Honolulu house.

Grandmother met us on her front lanai. "Just imagine," she said, "you left Maui only this morning, and here you are, the very same day, in time for tea."

After the long dusty drive, grandmother's breezy Honolulu house seemed restful and cool. The floors were all *lauhala* mats, the windows all screen, no glass. But here were the familiar old volcano pictures on the wall, and her big square grand piano in the living room. And then, how exciting, from her upstairs lanai I could hear the lion's roaring and see the trees of the Honolulu Zoo.

Our two weeks on Oahu passed all too soon.

Then, the take-off for Maui was the landing in reverse.

We said farewell on the splintery dock, eased ourselves into a canoe again, and were paddled off across the Pearl City lagoon. To me the seaplane looked like a giant winged water-spider trembling with eagerness to gulp us down and be gone.

Part way out, a regal lady passenger wearing a fine-woven *lauhala* hat with a blue peacock-feather lei, leaned forward and tapped the front paddler with her carved ivory fan. Without losing a stroke, we circled back to our still-waving families.

At the wooden steps a man lowered a large coconut-frond basket to the regal lady. As we backed away once more, she let me look. There, netted in the bottom of the basket, were two small brown hens.

Again we were on our way.

Hens and people were transferred from canoe to aircraft without dignity. I ascended variously placed footrests up the side of the hull, and descended into the barrel-like interior. Since there was only one seat on each side along the aisle, each passenger had a window.

The waves clapped against the hull in which we were encapsulated. The overhead engines whined and coughed, then roared with authority, our bones and voices vibrating as a part of the whole aircraft as we rocked forward.

Accelerating gradually, we planed a long way along the wave tops, the jolting slaps against the bottom of our hull increasing in tempo, until at last we seemed to shake free—and there!

There below was the green and white shoreline of Waikiki and Koko Head, fading into the green and brown of canefields and mountains and the blue and white of ocean and cloud. We passed over the red-brown island of Molokai, and already, far ahead we could see, looming up out of the clouds ahead, the long purple dome of Maui's Haleakala.

THE MANICURE

Under the fluorescent pink light
Aunt May contemplates her hands,
(Tomorrow, her grandson's wedding.)
Freckled, gnarled, calloused,
the broken nails defy
any hope of approval
from the supercilious manicurist.

"What," the pompommed voice shrills,
glossy scarlet-tipped fingers
clacking tall-stoppered bottles
against the slick plastic desk,
"have you been doing with these hands?"

Aunt May turns her hands palms up,
the long scar down her thumb
evidence of her ordeal
with an angry-fanged
barbed wire fence
that had trapped a neighbor's colt.

These callouses were toughened
by the stone wall she'd built,
now holding back a hill
beside a stream
where rainbow guppies swim,
heedless of their gaunt goddess
who guarded a world for them.

She'd planted trees alongside,
grown tall enough since then
to catch the rain
and bend the wind.

Her freckles, her grandson said,
were like sprinkles of cinnamon.

And she could braid a lariat,
and weave leis and mats,
and play the piano and viola,
the autoharp and harmonica,
and paint landscapes and ceilings,
hook a rug and gentle a mule,
train a vine without bruising it,
and fix the roof and feed the yearlings,

and at tea time,
when she arrived home, tooting the horn
of her sporty red Chevrolet,
Old Brown Dog,
and the cats and the donkey
and her neighbors came running to her
with glad cries.

Now Aunt May looks
into the uncurious eyes
of the svelte nail-polisher
and tries
to imagine what else SHE did
with her hands.

MAKENA SHARK GOD

It was still dark when Palani, white-haired *paniolo,* wisest of ranch men, was swinging open the corral gate. I rushed to ease the bridle over Ehu's velvety ears, to shorten stirrups, and stow my ration of rice balls and hard poi in my saddle bag. This was long ago, long before big Matson barges could guarantee safe transport of heavy cargo. And it was also my first lesson in insurance.

"Haay-yoop!" an aunty shouted, and the small herd of cattle ambled out into the Ulupalakua dawn and plodded down the road like a rippling stream of shadows flowing through the grove of giant trees.

The cattle seemed to enjoy themselves, occasionally mooing melodiously, padding along amiably as the dogs in the powdery dust. On we went, past ancient stone walls, past the tall eucalyptus forest, winding around the round grassy hills, and on, rhythmically, quietly, stirring variegated perfumes through the last of the night.

There was no hurry. The stars blazed in a sky more silver than black, and I felt proud and grown-up in my borrowed roping saddle.

The soft dust road became a gritty, stony trail. Curving turns became hairpin turns. Gradually the sky darkened to blue. The pounded-out trail became visible, a smooth grey line through the jagged lava. Trees were small, spiky, and scarce. Behind us, smoky clouds hid Haleakala's summit. Before us, more sloping miles tilted down toward the purple ocean.

The sun rose. The air grew warm. Cattle and horses poured along the road, brown and steaming. Lava outcrops jutted up, black and sharp, and the trail lurched down joltingly. *Panini* cactus was plentiful, fiercely thorny, but there was little other green tempting the cattle to stray.

On we went. The sun smote the black lava but the long simmering brown line continued along in its own contrapuntal rhythm.

The trail became sandy. The sun was still hot, but now *kiawe* trees screened the glare. More *kiawe* trees; taller, greener, almost enough for shade.

Grass appeared in tufts between the rocks. There was the smell of the ocean and drying seaweed, then a fence post, stone walls, a corral. Makena.

We guided the cattle into the shady corral, turned on a faucet over an old bathtub serving as a drinking trough, and left them to cool off.

I helped collect driftwood along the beach. Aunty and two *paniolos* clambered out to the end of a lava spit and tossed lines into the water. After a while one *paniolo* hauled in a fish, a medium sized *ulua.* Aunty rolled up her line and scooped a handful of crusty sea salt from a hollow in a wave-sprayed rock.

It all seemed so simple. Porous sea-worn stones were stacked for a fireplace. A pot of rice steamed over the driftwood fire. The fresh-caught *ulua* was plenty for all, and in those innocent times, sleeping between sand and stars held little danger except from centipedes and crabs.

Next morning, in the dim dawn, Palani showed me some blossoming papaya plants. Aunty helped me string two leis on the wispy ribs of palm fronds. And then Palani and I went quietly along the beach to a lava bluff, not really a cliff but high enough to call for cautious climbing.

Palani climbed up first. I watched him place an orange and a little sack of Bull Durham tobacco into a tiny cave. Then he jumped down and I scrambled up.

There he was. *Akua Mano,* the shark god, a small wooden image with chips of shell outlining his fierce upside down mouth. Arranged before him were two rice balls on a papaya leaf, a bottle of strawberry soda pop, Palani's sack of tobacco, and the orange.

Wordlessly, politely, I encircled these offerings with my two leis.

Then, suddenly I noticed it; there behind the wooden image, behind a dark overhang, smooth and black as onyx, a torpedo-shaped stone, longer than my arm. Without really knowing why, my hand went to my pocket and extracted the treasured Kalakaua quarter the tooth fairy had given me a few years before. It was my special lucky quarter but another glance into the niche decided me and I pressed the coin into the sand deep beneath the offerings.

The sun rose. And there was the inter-island steamer, *Humu'ula,* lurching off shore in deep water. We returned to join a busy scene.

Two whaleboats were approaching from the ship. Just beyond the shore breakers, the sailors backed oars and waited. In the corral the *paniolos* roped a steer by the horns, and before it had a chance to argue, "HoooooeeHAH!" out went the steer, herded between two horsemen, thundering across the beach and charging through the line of breaking surf. A rope was snapped to the sailors and the steer was lashed up against the side of the boat by the horns. Five more steers were hustled out, lashed securely, and the crew churned off for the ship.

For other kinds of trips, the island crews I'd met rowed in a relaxed style, chatting and enjoying the view on the way. Today, however, their oars beat double time, sending the boat lurching up under a wide hammock-like sling which hung from the ship's cargo boom.

Hastily the sling was cinched under the belly of a steer, and WHOOOSH! up he went, bawling and kicking, to the deck. At once the sling was yanked off and dropped to the whaleboat for the next steer. As the last steer rose toward the *Humu'ula's* deck, the boat turned about and surfed the swells toward the dusty cloud that billowed from the corral.

Aunty told me how sometimes the cattle on shore would decide to swim out to sea on their own. So I was assigned to ride Ehu through the breaking waves as one of the outriders.

There was shouting and splashing, but none of the familiar joking and laughing that usually accompanied cattle drives. Even from shore I could sense the tension aboard the *Humu'ula.* No one lounged along the railings today. Those not running or hauling or slamming pen gates were hanging from the rigging, looking out to sea. Even the rails on the side away from the loading were lined with watchers.

"How many more? How many now?" shouted the incoming boat crew. Ehu, too, was edgy. Though she was a veteran of many a cattle drive, she refused to swim past the breakers. Again and again she lunged for the shore.

"How many more? How many more?" the boatmen shouted. What were they expecting?

Then came a cry from up in the rigging. *"Akahele! Malama! Hemo na pipi!"* "Watch out! Take away the cattle!" Winches screamed. Men shouted. The last steer from the boat at shipside was heaved up in a snorting kicking swoop. The outgoing boat swirled around and rowed mightily back to the shallows, where the last six steers were untied, hustled ashore, and herded tightly back into the stone coral. Ehu bolted for the beach where we joined the others on the sand, staring seaward to where it seemed every hand aboard the *Humu'ula* was pointing.

"There!" Aunty waved toward the reef. Then I saw it too, the thin black fin, like a scimitar, slicing the surface, drifting smoothly. Another fin. Two more.

The fins wandered away, then returned, cruising parallel with the line of surf. Gradually their zigzagging course brought them nearer, and through the foam-topped, translucent waves we could see their dark torpedo shapes.

Palani rode up, his big mare snorting and wet. *"Maikai,"* he said. "Good. Only six steers left. We send by truck to Kahului." He smiled. *"Akua Mano* feeling friendly today. Nobody hurt. Lucky."

Years later I visited the shark god's cave at Makena. I had a hard time finding it even though no hotels had yet sprung up. The wooden image was gone. But dimly discernible, far back in its niche, the torpedo shape was still there. And just inside the opening, I saw a dried crown-flower lei, a can of orange soda pop and, on a plastic plate, two fresh donuts.

I dug my fingers in the sand beneath the plastic plate. There it was—the old Kalakaua quarter, a valuable addition to my collection.

But then I heard my children splashing and shouting in the waves. Another glance at the fierce form of *Akua Mano* decided me. Very respectfully I replaced the rare quarter. Very respectfully I buried a new silver Eisenhower dollar beside it. And then, even so, just to be sure, I called my children ashore to play on the sand.

When I last visited Makena, hotels covered the old landmarks. I saw no sign of the little cave. And neither ships nor sharks come now to add excitement to those newly-tamed waters.

P.M.F.

AUNT MINA

Aunt Mina,
alone in November fog at the mountain house,
made Mina Mints for Christmas–
her recipe a secret: mint and lemon and lime,
like puffs of spicy breeze.

She wore child-sized shoes
and prim brown dresses,
and respect for her was mandatory.

In late summer, also, she went alone.
Such a scandal at that time
of sternly sequestered Proper Women,
Yet, stubbornly, this straight-backed rebel,
left husband and five children
firmly behind.

Wandering close along the boundary line,
sidling along the thorny pathways,
hair mist-frosted, haloed by sun,
with only strong pony,
many birds, and her song,
Aunt Mina picked blackberries.

She made Good jellies, and Proper jars of jam,
quaintly labeled, very respectable,
commendable jars of jams and jellies.

And still she picked blackberries,
quarts and quarts of blackberries,
crammed them in the long yellow
claw-footed bathtub,
and as the summer neared the fall,
Aunt Mina, strong-willed wife
of a missionary son,
made wine.

OBAA SAN

Obaa san,
born daughter of a strong,
frightened hoe-*hana* lady on Molokai,
by light of kerosene lanterns
and stars–

She holds now
the small sure hand
of her visiting granddaughter,
born daughter of a strong,
enlightened computer operator,
in the sterile glare
of many prismed lights
of Kapiolani Hospital.

They cross the road together
and pause beneath a street light
to examine the child's drawing,
a flattened dome on the flat pale page.

"See, *Obaa san*.
My teacher say this very very good."

"Aaah? You peetchah-make gurassu housu?"

"No, no. Not a grass house.
This is my house for when
I get big like my mama."

"But, hai yah!
No moa tree? No moa flowah?"

"Course not.
Don't you know anything?
This is a solar habitat. For when
I live on the moon."

She flounces off alert
to the calls of a child-friend,
her *zori* beating rhythmic,
her pony-tail pert.

The tiny grandmother,
skilled at saddling mules at dawn,
and catching *ulua*
from a Kihei reef by torch light,
who can name the stars in Hawaiian
and English and Japanese,
bends stiffly, and kneels,
haloed by the glow from Paia Store,
to retrieve the child's drawing
where it was flung carelessly
in the dirt.

HAMAKUAPOKO

Up the soft-dust road they came,
quietly, through margins of sun and moon,
first the young-folk and the dogs,
then the mama-*sans* with their babies
and grass mats and *zabuton,*
then the hoe-*hana* men and Domingo's donkey,
these villagers from a once real town
now plowed-under cane fields, and
vanished like Brigadoon.

Surrounded by sugar cane,
narrow ditches and sky,
they were walking to this home
with many wide windows
and eight plank steps before an open lanai.

Plantation seasons sectioned out the long year:
after torches and cinders,
the red dust of plowing,
then the view of the sea from the high lanai.

Then the seed-cane furrows,
and the seed-cane planting,
and the seed-cane sprouting,
and the *hana-wai* flumes
along the earth-red rows.

Then the green cane growing
clear up to the yard fence,
then all the view erased from the wide lanai.

Then man-tall tall, the purple-furred tassels.
Then the drying-out weeks.
Then the oiled burlap torches,
and the flames and the shouting,
and the cane leaves burning,

and again the furrowed land
and the red dust of plowing.

All the years this vanished town
had lived its life in these patterned rhythms.
(Rise before the rumble
of the plantation engines,
Pau hana time when the last train would go.
Thoughts with the dirt,
with the seed-cane sections,
with the Friday pay envelope,
and the evening *furo*.)

And then one evening of mysterious plan,
from the edge of the village
came new-patterned rhythms.
Miss Curtis had arrived
with her grand square grand.

And then came interludes rare and elusive,
fleeting as mongooses, remembered like perfume,
when no roaring cane fires
burned the evening black,
when the moon would be full,
and no clouds dripped mud,
then the children ran to ask her,
(well, they asked Bella to ask her)
and hearing her answer,
raced importantly back–

"Miss Curtis will play tonight
on her grand square grand."

Oh I remember how swiftly
they came through the yard gate,
how I ran out to meet them
down the eight plank steps,

how the moon rose softly, as we all had wished,
how we rolled out our mats on the springy grass,
how Ah Sing lit mosquito punk,
and Bella brought lamps,
and they centered the piano
above the eight plank steps.

And Aunt Nell lit candles
in the filigreed holders,
and they pushed the doors aside
on the wide lanai.

Then the hoe-*hana* men in starch-ironed shirts,
their hair slicked down,
leaned along the yard fence,
and little clumps of young folk
sat demure and quiet,
and the dogs and the donkey
roamed free in the shadows,

and stately Miss Curtis
came out to greet her audience.

There were no programs. No one clapped.
But perfumes of yellow soap,
nasturtiums and hair-oil,
eucalyptus and camphor
and garlic and guava,
were mixed with jasmine.
And the small breeze
breathed its blessing over all of us.

Oh I see her still, tall in the moonlight,
a slim, unusual woman
in her same ivory lace
she'd kept from her young age,

when she'd played the Brahms concertos
with the San Francisco symphony.
But now she spoke of courage,
of grief endured with grace,
of Chopin's box of home-earth,
his cherished soil of Poland.

And the solemn village elders,
(their earth-jars in their shrines nearby)
sighed for Chopin, and Miss Curtis.
They knew she too was far from her homeland.
And distanced like theirs by newer ties.

First, she played them lullabies,
till the babies slept, soft on the *zabuton*.
And then– waltzes for the young,
and mazurkas and polkas.
For Aunt Nell, she played Chopin,
For me, she played Czerny.
For us all she played Beethoven,
Tchaikovsky and Brahms,
and then at the last, (perhaps for herself?)
the heart-lifting thunders of Liszt.

Oh, I see us all still, bright in the moonlight,
as we heard the last long, great chords fade,
and, still at the keyboard, how she would wait
while the villlagers rolled up their mats to go,

how their last shy goodbyes
were waved from the yardgate,

how I stayed behind in the flattened grass
as they passed on in silence
down the star-curtained road.

The dust rose again from the Paia plains.
The candles were snuffed.
She left the lanai.

Then I felt the thick chill fog
slink down from Makawao,
and dim the moon into
mist.

PARABLE OF THE ONION

The new yardman's truck swooped up Aunt Winnie's driveway and parked. A young man jumped down. Then his pretty wife climbed out on the other side calling out, "Now you two be good," as she did. With a quick smile to Aunt Winnie, they hoisted out rakes and a lawn mower.

As Aunt Winnie and I approached the truck cab, two little girls holding pencils and drawing pads met our gaze. Aunt Winnie waved to their parents. "Mind if they come out and sit under my tree? I'll watch them," she added quickly.

The mother waved back and disappeared around the corner of the house.

Aunt Winnie moved into the shade of her old *kukui* tree and seated herself against its friendly trunk. "Let's see your drawings," she said with an encouraging nod.

The older child approached diffidently and held out her sketch pad. "What a smart mother," Aunt Winnie said. "Blank pages so her daughter can try her own ideas." One of the pages held the drawing of a smiling face with the name under it. Rosalani. And in a frame all around the face was a border of brightly crayoned flowers.

"How pretty," said Aunt Winnie. "Rosalani. Is this your name? Rosalani?"

"No, that's my sister's name. I'm Maude. That's me down there."

We looked where the small nail-bitten finger was pointing to a brown snowman shaped figure squeezed between two of the border plants, and looked quizzically into the serious brown eyes of the dark-browed child before us.

"I'm brown because my name sounds like mud, and . . ." The small hand dug a tiny stony-looking object from the grass and rubbed the dirt from it with her thumb.

"When I was little," Aunt Winnie said "One of my best friends was Maude. And she was beautiful. Like you." She paused but the brown eyes were on the muddy thing clenched in her hand. "And you, Rosalani," Aunt Winnie added, turning to the blond smiling child sitting tight beside Maude, "you are beautiful too."

For a while we four sat in companionable quiet listening to the birds chattering at Aunt Winnie's cat, who had stalked over to display his indifference to us.

Then Rosalani asked, "Can you tell stories?"

"Well," Aunt Winnie said, "I know one about a girl who wanted a cat, but I'd need a pencil and some paper." Maude turned to a clean page on her sketch pad. Rosalani offered a nubbin of crayon. The girls slid closer.

"Once upon a time. . ." Aunt Winnie began.

Just then Mrs. Rowan from across the road walked up the driveway. Aunt Winnie beckoned to her. "We're just about to start a story." she explained. "Come join us."

Mrs. Rowan sat beside Rosalani on the grass.

Both children stared at her.

"She has even more wrinkles than you," Rosalani said wonderingly to Aunt Winnie.

"My mother says," Maude told us, "everything has a because. Why does she have such deep lines in her face?"

"Because she's been beautiful a longer time than you," said Aunt Winnie as Mrs. Rowan's chin went down and her eyes looked at her hands.

"I don't understand," said Rosalani.

"Look at Haleakala over there," said Aunt Winnie.

Five of us now turned to observe.

The great mountain, clear against the smooth blue sky, lifted lavender and pink in the early light, its long sloping sides ruggedly crevassed above its morning lei of bubble-shaped clouds.

"Haleakala's really really old, isn't it," Maude breathed wonderingly. "Are you really really old too?"

"Only on the outside."

"What do you mean?" Maude looked up sharply.

"Like an onion," said Aunt Winnie.

"I don't understand that either," Rosalani said. "Onions are brown and crinkly." She giggled and looked sideways at Maude.

"Crinkly brown on the outside," Aunt Winnie explained. "Then layers inside secret layers of interesting mystery, all mooncolor and smooth until you reach the most inside part, and that's a green surprise waiting to be put into the magic mud to grow."

Maude sighed, "Magic mud." Turning to Mrs. Rowan she asked "Are you old like that? Are you really really old?"

"Only my shell," Mrs. Rowan said. And suddenly her smile lit up her green-blue eyes, and the sunlight glowed so cheerily on her springy white hair that Maude smiled in return.

"I know." Maude said. "Like this *kukui* seed." She held out her small browny-black lump. "All interesting wrinkles on the outside. See?" She put the seed in Mrs. Rowan's hand. "But there's a secret tree-to-be, all moon-color-new, tight inside." She glanced shyly up at Mrs. Rowan. "I'm going to be a botanist when I grow up. Like my mother," she added hastily, and looked hard at Rosalani. "I think *kukui* seeds and onions are beautiful," she said. "Don't you?"

"Uh huh," Rosalani replied, "but mud is more interesting." She took the seed Mrs. Rowan passed to her and admired it politely. "It's mud that's really magic," she argued. "Mud can turn crinkly things into flowers. And turn tiny seeds into big trees for birds to sit on." Then she looked at Maude. "Mud is beautiful too," she said very firmly. "I like mud."

PROPERTY TAXES

The woodrose veiled the only line
between Aunt Winnie's home and mine.

The trail once curved between the stones
of ancient walls. Now clumps of stumps
are all I see
of Aunty's once-towering mango trees.

I feel again the wild hard thumps
of cardboard sleds, and finger the scars
of cuts and scrapes on toes and elbows
as I hear the indifferent dump trucks growl.

I look up on that bull-dozed hill
and think I never have known a pain
as sharp and hard as this new loss
of birds and trees and home for owls
and wide lanais and welcome shouts
from up that hill.

And now the rain brings mud and weeds
in gouging slides instead of blessing
to the pond and garden once so green
up on that hill,

and my aunty, my friend, has gone away
to a concrete condo against her will.

PLANTATION THEATER ARTS

"Don't sit in front of third graders or hair-oil heads," we'd whisper to each other as we entered the old Hamakuapoko theater.

That was way back when we were the know-it-alls of small-town Maui. We knew how a nearby viewer's gardenia hair pomade would permeate even our own hair, so that next day Mrs. Glick would know we'd gone to a movie instead of doing homework. We also knew that third graders kicked the seats all through the show.

In today's theaters we are insulated from the world in sound-proofed, air-conditioned buildings. But when I was a kid, the audience, the buildings themselves, and all the surrounding world were part of the performance.

Action at Hamakuapoko was fairly typical. You never heard of Hamakuapoko? Well, fields of cane grow now where once there were homes and buildings and a railroad depot.

That theater was a popular place. Five cents got you a seat on a bench or on your own mat or newspaper up front on the chunked-up floor. Ten cents got you a folding chair in the middle. There was also a loge section. The loge seats were three broken-down sofas in the back. They were alive with fleas so no one sat there except the dogs and first-timers.

In big town Paia, the theater stood right beside the mill. It was more sophisticated. Fewer dogs. Bigger. But seat selection demanded the same cool plantation-town know-how.

First rule was don't come too early. Wait till the others quit running around collecting friends. Then you knew where the perfumed heads and seat-kickers were. Seats with the best view were in back of loving couples. They usually snuggled way down, so it was easy to see over their heads.

Some theaters had windows along the sides. Tobacco spitters sat by windows. Buildings with windows were crowded in the center, but safer.

If there was a balcony, however, the center front was risky. You could get zinged from upstairs with chewed *si mui* seeds, and if you got stuck in the row just under the balcony edge, you would be in a light but steady rain of pumpkin-seed and pine-nut hulls. You combed your hair mighty carefully before your mom spied any chaff, or she'd make you shampoo with Fels Naptha, and that pungent yellow brick of laundry soap made your eyes sting like the dickens.

We used to snicker at the fools who parked themselves in back of empty seats. Just as the lights went out, sure enough, here would come a Hawaiian family. They were tall, usually wore wide brimmed hats with feather leis, and sat so straight most of us couldn't even see over their shoulders. There was usually a scramble to move somewhere in front of them.

Managers of two-price houses anticipated other kinds of migrations. They were about the same on all the islands. Here's the way my husband described a movie outing at Kaneohe, before WWII.

"We lived at Mokapu," he said, "where the Marine Base airplane runways are now, and the shortest way to Kaneohe was straight across the bay. So we chugged over in our motorboat, tied up at the old yacht-club pier, put the spark plug in a pocket, and hiked into Kaneohe town.

"Fifteen cent seats were in the middle, and had backs. Dime seats were benches. No backs. Most everyone bought dime tickets. When the lights went out, the bench crowd slithered over to the chairs. Blink! The lights went on. Everybody scurried back to the benches. Lights out—back to the seats. Lights on—again a retreat. After three or four times the manager quit and started the show."

Wise parents let their kids choose the seats. But any parent was boss of any kid. This hasn't changed entirely. Some time ago, I saw a hand-lettered sign posted by the ticket window of the only theater on the island of Lanai. It said

TWENTY ADULTS
OR NO SHOW

Seat selection accomplished, the audience watched the clock. The projectionist seldom did. So even a minute of delay triggered a storm of whistling and clapping. This is where

MAPUANA THEATER
ART IS LONG TIME IS FLEETING
ONE PICTURE IS WORTH A THOUSAND WORDS
TUES. NIGHT- BUCK ROGERS EPISODE #17 FOLLOWED BY BANK NITE! $'SS - PRIZES
M.G.M. PRESENTS... (AND) COMING SOON GARBO & GILBERT IN A NEW ONE!
PASSION'S PLAYTHING
ELGIN
SEPTEMBER
FOUND HAT
RIDERS OF SAGE
DOUBLE BILL NOW TOM MIX x 2
"RIDERS OF EL PASOBLE" AND CIMMARON SUNSET... COMING SOON!!
LOW ELLA'S LEIS
MAUNA LOA $2.00
AKULIKULI $3.95
(TUES. ONLY)
PRICES ADULTS 25¢ KIDS 15¢
SEKI KAUKAU (NEXT DOOR)
PEPEAU - 2 for 5¢
MANAPUA - 5¢
HOME-MADE MANGO SEED - BAG OR LB.
SHAVE ICE 5¢
CRACK SEED 5¢
NO DOGS INSIDE
5¢ LB.
P.M.F.

many of us developed style in whistling. Some kids whistled with two fingers, some just through their teeth. My father, like the Japanese and Chinese elders, sat in silent dignity. My mother didn't whistle, but she clapped in rhythm with the rest, and eventually heavy feet were heard pounding up the steps into the loft where the mysterious movie machine lurked.

The clapping and whistling continued however, until finally the whistling and yelling of "Ey! Saburo-*san*, wassamadda you!" achieved a shriek of orchestra noise, and a wavering image on the undulating screen. (In breezier places, scenery and characters remained in hula motion from the cartoon to THE END.) More shouting helped Saburo-*san* (or Henry or Moses) adjust focus and sound. "Turn 'em down!" "Too much!" "Up a leedle." "Okay-lie-dat." Then we'd settle back in weary triumph to enjoy the cartoon, newsreel and, if lucky, another cartoon, and the main feature, in that order.

Once the show got under way for sure, order was quickly established. If any jabbering was heard, the Portuguese elders went "ssssSSSSSSS!" The white-bearded Filipino grandfathers glared ferociously. And any jouncing kid in front of a Chinese grandmother would be subdued by a rap on the head with a clacking carved sandlewood fan.

Things worked out pretty well. The Hawaiians with their keen eyes usually sat toward the back. And there were enough Chinese matriarchs and other elders to glare and whack decent manners into those who needed them.

A plantation audience had to be alert. When sudden showers smote the iron roof, whether at Paia, Lahaina or Hamakuapoko, movie goers shouted anew for Saburo-*san* to "Turn 'em up!" But when the unseen rain cloud passed on, and the long thundering drumroll on the roof was suddenly silenced, the movie sound still bellowed. And then the yells arose again. "Turn 'em down, Saburo! Turn 'em down!"

The sound effects of today's electronic synthesizers, and cinerama's sensurround are true marvels, but many an iron roofed plantation movie house offered more than sound.

These iron roofs didn't just shed rain. They had personality and voice. The most versatile roofs were created with an open frame of wooden two-by-fours. Sheets of corrugated iron, eight feet long, were spiked to the wide spaced beams. The upper surface was roof; the underside was ceiling. Lizards whisked along the beams, their ''ChikChak!'' echoing loud as birds. This expanse of flexible iron amplified the sound of anything touching it.

Easily discernible, for example, was the fate of a centipede rustling frantically down an iron furrow, stalked by one of the ubiquitous free-flying Leghorn hens.

Tympanic effects varied according to season and setting. Consider these long resonant sheets under a giant mango tree, as small green mangoes, then big, then over-ripe, pinged, ponged, and plopped progressively all through the mango year.

The first time I saw Ginger Rogers and Fred Astaire, I thought their dancing somewhat over-rated. It was raining hard enough to drown out the orchestra, and they seemed oddly out of step with the thudding rhythms of wind-flailed palm fronds whanging against the metal eaves.

In more rainy districts, vines grew so fast they meshed trees and house together in a tight tough net. When the wind swayed the trees, the vines yanked at the eaves, dragged the flexible iron sheets up and down on their fastening nails, and grated the loosened plates against each other in shrieking, shivering protest. A tender love scene then, even between Clark Gable and Jean Harlow, became irresistible comedy.

As these roofs aged, the nails wore thinner and the holes larger, synthesizing even more intricate chords and squawks to orchestrate the settings of jungle and forest where roamed Tarzan or the last of the Mohicans, episode after episode, through the Saturday summer afternoons.

On a hot day an iron roof heated up like a griddle. Interesting jungle smells then steamed from the ripe mash of squashed mango, or guava, *lilikoi,* papaya, or combinations thereof.

Other special effects were produced when a roach-filled cluster of coconuts crashed like a bomb just overhead, its evicted millions of inhabitants pouring across the roof in a vast rustling wave, making us feel crawly all over.

Over the years, progress inflicted improvements. In town after town the shady trees were exterminated, exchanging aroma and shade for parking space and sauna bath atmosphere. When sudden showers smote these solar-heated roofs, the sizzling metal twanged and cracked like rifle shots.

In sugar-mill towns like Paia, there were other unique treats. Just a stone's throw from the movie screen were the mill's great humming flywheels and centrifuges, and the thundering washers and grinders.

In those days a loquacious steam engine dragged shrieking trainloads of cane to the mill (chuffa chuffa). Here it came. (chufa Chufff Haa, CHUFFF) "EH! Saburo-*san*! Turn-em UP!" (SSHHUFFFF Ttffff cheeuFFF SSSHHOOOoooooo) Then it was, "SABURO-*SAN!* TURN 'EM DOWN!"

Some people avoided mill-town movie houses during grinding season. But I loved the weird symphony of mill and train and iron roof rumbling in harmony with each other.

Of course if you scorned the sound effects of these special roofs, there were places only partly roofed. There, if you didn't like the movie, you could watch the stars and moon overhead. On wet nights however, you crowded under the roof and watched the movie through a curtain of rain.

All the movie palaces I remember were equally well air-conditioned with real air. One I liked especially had no sidewalls except for a barbed wire pasture fence. Dogs, chickens, sometimes a goat, strolled casually in and out. When the rooster crowed from the screen to announce the Pathe News, he was challenged by the sleepy but conscientious fighting cocks perched on the fence railing behind the last row.

Was eating as much a part of the movie ritual then as it is today? Yes, indeed. But popcorn? Cokes in plastic cups? Not then.

We were equipped with a dime, a nickel, and an empty envelope. The dime bought admission. The nickel bought a small brown paper sack, brim full of crackseed, pine nuts, or *si mui*. The envelope, a courtesy to the barefoot majority, was to spit the seeds in. If we forgot the envelope, we bought *iriko*. Salty, chewy, no seeds.

Today, some theaters offer art exhibits to entertain the patrons before the show. They remind me again of Hamakuapoko's movie palace. The screen was a cotton sheet. After every rain its mildew patterns changed and grew. We called it action art. Like a Rorschach picture test, it inspired discussion, until one day, Bella, who made the best Portuguese sweet bread in the village, stomped up after THE END, snatched down the sheet, and returned it washed, starch-ironed, and smelling of Clorox, in time for the next show. For some weeks after, the pictures all seemed to move through a grid of sharp, square crease lines.

Going home from an evening show was another adventure. Even in Wailuku, Maui's big town in those days, the street lights were turned off at nine o'clock, and movie goers exited blindly into the dark to hunt for their own cars by feeling the hood ornaments of the automobiles lined up along the town's main street.

Proper theater etiquette was demonstrated by the first finders, who turned on their headlights, backed out into the street, and remained there with their light beams aimed along the sidewalk so others could find their way as far as Ichiki Store. Here the generous family left the light bulb in the front store window glowing all night. It served as a landmark for the main street and a beacon for all.

I remember my first visit to Honolulu's new Waikiki Theater. The program? I forget. It was the theater itself we talked about. Ooh! Ah! Oh, the rainbow of colored lights, the realistic rubber banana plants along the walls, the cloud effects, and the twinkling ceiling lights, like stars! The luminescent flower pattern on the soft carpet illuminated the aisles even after the house lights went out. And when Ed Sawtelle played that super organ before the movie began, the rainbow colors changed, and the cloud effects moved across the ceiling!

And yet, there comes that catch at the heart when I recall the real trees of Hamakuapoko and Lahaina, the real birds rattling seeds onto the musical roofs, the real stars illuminating our aisles and paths and the village audience, and all the cool perfumed world around us, the motherly ticket sellers at the window, and the newsy signs and local offerings for sale near the entrance.

"Never mind what the movie is," my grandmother used to say. "Go see the whole show."

I didn't understand what she really meant then. But I think I do now.

P.M.F.

A LEGACY

According to some people,
life is merely something that goes along
like a string of knots.
They feel along
bump
by
bump
over
each knot
until
there
is
an
end,
and
that
is
THE END.

Some people do live their lives
like that. Struggling
bump
by
root
by
stone
by
turn,
their
object,
to
get
to
SOMETHING or SOMEPLACE.

Their first knot is the beginning.
The last is the end.

Maybe they're right. Maybe so.
And yet– it's the going–
the going itself is adventure for me.

I breathe the air Kaahumanu breathed.
I sing the songs of Liliuokalani.

I walk these trails my mother walked,
and eat the fruit from trees that grew
from seeds her grandma planted here.

I fling my seeds. They'll grow tall trees.
My grandson's sons will eat from these.

GLOSSARY

AE Yes.

AIA There; there you have it; there you are.

AKAHELE Go carefully; beware.

AKUA A god or goddess; gods, spirit, ghost. In Hawaii, trees, waterfalls, mountains, valleys, rocks, and people and other creatures all have their own akua. Some -- the shark, for instance -- are very powerful.

AUWE Exclamation of dismay; alas.

EHU Sand color; reddish.

FURO Japanese hot tub.

GEKKO A small grey lizard.

GETA Japanese wooden clogs.

HAKU Woven.

HANA-WAI Hana, work; wai, water. The hana-wai man is the irrigation worker who deals with ditches and flumes.

HELE MAI Come here. Hele, to walk or move or go; mai, this way.

HEMO Take away.

HIROGANA A form of Japanese writing using syllable characters.

HOE-HANA A pidgin term for working with the hoe; colloquialism for manual labor. Hana means work; the hoe here is just a hoe.

HUHU Anger; displeasure; scolding; wrath. To provoke anger, or pretend anger.

HUKI-POLE This is a springy carrying pole for divided loads. Buckets or bundles of nearly equal weight are slung at each end and the pole is balanced across one shoulder. The experienced load bearer has a jouncy walk, his or her feet moving in time with each upswing of the pole.

IRIKO A Japanese term for tiny dried fish.

KEIKI Child. Ke, the; iki, little or small.

KIAWE Also known as algaroba or mesquite. A thorny tree with tiny leaves and long sweet-tasting yellow beans.

KIMONO Japanese outer garment usually worn with deep flowing sleeves.

KUKUI Light, torch, or lamp; the candlenut tree. Kukui groves appear luminescent, the first visible in the valleys at dawn, the last discernible at night. The oily nuts were used for candles, medicine, and wood finishing; polished shells for ornaments.

LANAI Veranda or porch.

LAUHALA Leaf of the hala, or pandanus, tree.

LEI Wreath of flowers and/or foliage.

LILIKOI Passionflower vine. Variations have yellow or purple juicy, egg-shaped fruit.

MAIKAI Good.

MALAMA Beware.

MANO Shark.

MANUA Fertilizer. From the word "manure."

MAUKA Toward the mountain.

MILO A native Hawaiian tree with small leaves and pale hard wood.

NAUPAKA A shrub with white berries.

OBAA-SAN Japanese term meaning respected grandmother.

OBI Japanese word for sash.

OHELO A high altitude shrub, with red or white berries, said to be sacred to Pele, the goddess of volcanoes.

PANINI Cactus.

PANIOLO Cowboy. From the word Espanol, the expert horsemen from Spain.

PAU HANA Pau, finished, the end; hana, work.

PILI A tall tough grass, useful for thatching.

PIPI Beef, cattle. From the word beef.

POI A staple food made from pounded taro root.

PUNE'E A couch.

SAN A Japanese term of respect or endearment.

SENSEI Japanese word for teacher.

SI MUI Chinese dried plum or cherry preserved with salt, sugar and spices.

TARO Food plant. Its purplish-grey root bulb is steamed then pounded with water to make poi. The young leaves, well cooked, are like spinach.

TATAMI Japanese grass mat.

TI A native plant whose long shiny leaves are used for cooking, medicine, religious rites, and decoration.

ULUA A large edible fish.

ZABUTON Japanese word for a flat, square floor cushion, usually about a yard square.

ZORI Japanese slipper.

A pencil sketch of the author by the illustrator on a hike in 1974.